This journal is all about:

Breed:

Age when I brought you home:

Birthday:

my adorable CAT

A Journal & Keepsake Book

CHRONICLE BOOKS

SAN FRANCISCO

Manufactured in China.

Designed by Brooke Johnson and Jon Glick.
Illustrations by Melissa Chaib.

10 9 8 7 6 5 4 3 2 1

Chronicle Books LLC
680 Second Street
San Francisco, CA 94107
www.chroniclebooks.com

Contents

our
cat is
adorable!

Meow

Introduction

Maybe you just brought your fur baby home, or maybe your kitty has been part of the family for years now. No matter what, this keepsake journal is the perfect place to capture all those memories and milestones, firsts and favorites, with the most fabulous cat (yours, of course). Paste in photos to remember the good times (snuggles in bed) and the bad (demolished the couch arm), the significant events (first birthday), and the everyday moments (all those naps) you never want to forget. Take time to note all of the things that make your precious kitty like no other and all the stories that make you smile.

How
We
Met

_____

_____

_____

_____

_____

_____

_____

_____

_____

_____

_____

_____

_____

_____

_____

_____

Date: _____

I knew you were my baby as soon as . . . **PURR**

_____

_____

_____

_____

_____

_____

_____

_____

_____

_____

[paste your photo here]

The Story of Your Name

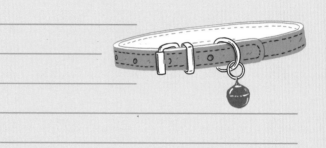

I almost named you:

All of Your Nicknames

Favorite nickname:

All
about
You

It makes me laugh when you . . .

_____

_____

_____

I call you a good cat when you . . .

_____

_____

_____

I call you a bad cat when you . . .

_____

_____

_____

I love it when you . . .

_____

_____

_____

You are:

Soft	Snuggly	Aloof
Wiry	Lazy	**Independent**
Puffy	A purrer	Neurotic
Sleek	**An angel**	Energetic
Floofy	A menace	A wild beast
Graceful	**A genius**	**Classy**
Funny	A dum-dum	A pouncer
Crazy	A good cuddler	**A prancer**
Sassy	**A stinker**	**A jumper**
Scaredy	A goofball	A climber
Adventurous	Refined	**The boss**

More about You

Foods that you love:

_____

_____

_____

Average hours spent sleeping a day:

_____

_____

_____

Your most lovable time of day:

_____

_____

_____

Paw prints

Tail

On your best days, you look like this:

[paste your photo here]

But when you wake up with your fur all askew,
you still look adorable:

[paste your photo here]

Some of your favorite spots to lounge are:

[paste your photo here]

[paste your photo here]

Firsts

First day at your forever home:

_____

_____

_____

_____

[paste your photo here]

First visit to the vet:

GOOD
KITTY

_____

_____

_____

First boo-boo:

_____

_____

_____

First hair ball:

_____

_____

_____

[paste your photo here]

First nail-clipping session:

_____

_____

_____

First run-in with water:

_____

_____

_____

First brushing:

_____

_____

_____

[paste your photo here]

First toy:

_____

_____

_____

First scratching post:

_____

_____

_____

First holiday celebration:

_____

_____

_____

[paste your photo here]

How We Celebrated Your First Birthday

What we did:

_____

_____

_____

Who came:

_____

_____

_____

What you ate:

_____

_____

_____

Party date:

_____

Other Firsts

Write in your own firsts with your cat on the lines below.

Favorites

Favorite treats:

_____

_____

_____

Favorite games:

_____

_____

_____

Favorite sun spots:

_____

_____

_____

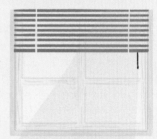

Favorite way to fall asleep:

[paste your photo here]

Favorite TV show to watch:

_____

_____

_____

Favorite humans (other than your parents):

_____

_____

_____

Favorite way to get someone's attention:

_____

_____

_____

Favorite places to be scratched/tickled/rubbed:

_____

_____

_____

Favorite place to sit:

_____

_____

_____

Favorite toy to play with:

_____

_____

_____

Favorite thing to chew on:

_____

_____

_____

Favorite games:

_____

_____

_____

Favorite naughty thing to do:

_____

_____

_____

Other Favorites

Write in your own favorites with your cat
on the lines below.

_____

_____

_____

_____

_____

_____

_____

_____

_____

_____

_____

_____

_____

Feelings

You are not a fan of:

_____

_____

_____

Neighborhood enemy (or enemies):

_____

_____

_____

Feelings about dogs:

_____

_____

_____

Feelings about birds and other wild animals that appear
out the window:

_____

_____

_____

Feelings about small children:

_____

_____

_____

Feelings about the doorbell:

_____

_____

_____

Feelings about people shoes:

_____

_____

_____

Feelings about people eating:

_____

_____

_____

Feelings about car rides:

_____

_____

_____

Feelings about leashes and carriers:

_____

_____

_____

Feelings about the vet:

_____

_____

_____

Feelings about outside:

_____

_____

_____

Feelings about brushing and nail clipping:

_____

_____

_____

Feelings about appliances that make noise
(the dishwasher, the washing machine, etc.):

_____

_____

_____

Feelings about other cats:

_____

_____

_____

Feelings about the weird cat in the mirror:

_____

_____

_____

Feelings about kittens:

_____

_____

_____

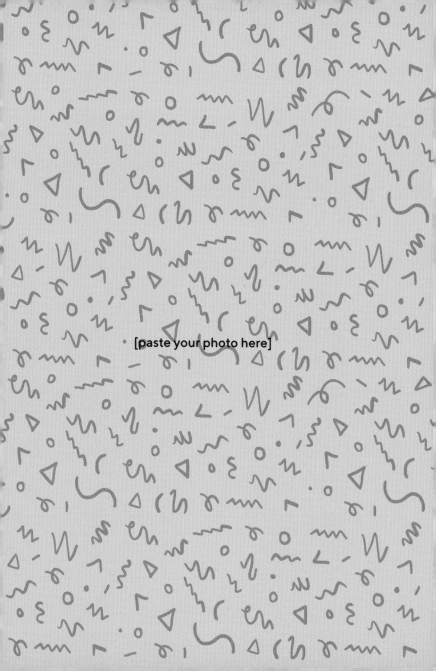
[paste your photo here]

Annoyances

The things I do that annoy you the most:

_____

_____

_____

_____

_____

_____

_____

_____

_____

_____

_____

_____

_____

_____

Things you've destroyed:

_____

_____

_____

[paste your photo here]

Things you've tried to eat:

_____

_____

_____

[paste your photo here]

Things you've tried to drink out of:

_____

_____

_____

[paste your photo here]

The annoying things you do (but I still love you):

_____

_____

_____

[paste your photo here]

You're good/bad at sharing. . .

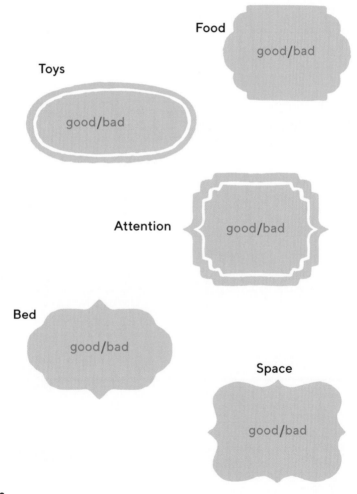

Food

good/bad

Toys

good/bad

Attention

good/bad

Bed

good/bad

Space

good/bad

But how can I resist this face:

[paste your photo here]

Our
Best
Selfies

[paste your photos here]

[paste your photos here]

[paste your photos here]

[paste your photos here]

[paste your photos here]

[paste your photos here]

[paste your photos here]

[paste your photos here]

[paste your photos here]

[paste your photos here]

[paste your photos here]

[paste your photos here]

[paste your photos here]

[paste your photos here]

[paste your photos here]

[paste your photos here]

[paste your photos here]

[paste your photos here]

[paste your photos here]

[paste your photos here]

[paste your photos here]

[paste your photos here]

Stories
&
Memories

Remember when we . . . ?

_____

_____

_____

_____

_____

_____

_____

_____

_____

_____

_____

_____

_____

_____

_____

_____

There was that time we . . .

_____

_____

_____

_____

_____

_____

_____

_____

_____

_____

_____

_____

_____

_____

_____

_____

A great memory!

_____

_____

_____

_____

_____

_____

_____

_____

_____

_____

_____

_____

_____

_____

_____

_____

_____

Remember when we . . . ?

_____

_____

_____

_____

_____

_____

_____

_____

_____

_____

_____

_____

_____

_____

_____

_____

_____

_____

There was that time we . . .

_____

_____

_____

_____

_____

_____

_____

_____

_____

_____

_____

_____

_____

_____

_____

_____

A great memory!

_____

_____

_____

_____

_____

_____

_____

_____

_____

_____

_____

_____

_____

_____

_____

_____

_____

_____

Remember when we . . . ?

_____

_____

_____

_____

_____

_____

_____

_____

_____

_____

_____

_____

_____

_____

_____

_____

There was that time we . . .

_____

_____

_____

_____

_____

_____

_____

_____

_____

_____

_____

_____

_____

_____

_____

_____

A great memory!

_____

_____

_____

_____

_____

_____

_____

_____

_____

_____

_____

_____

_____

_____

_____

Remember when we . . . ?

_____

_____

_____

_____

_____

_____

_____

_____

_____

_____

_____

_____

_____

_____

_____

There was that time we . . .

A great memory!

_____

_____

_____

_____

_____

_____

_____

_____

_____

_____

_____

_____

_____

_____

_____

_____

Remember when we . . . ?

_____

_____

_____

_____

_____

_____

_____

_____

_____

_____

_____

_____

_____

_____

_____

_____

_____

There was that time we . . .

_____

_____

_____

_____

_____

_____

_____

_____

_____

_____

_____

_____

_____

_____

_____

_____

A great memory!

_____

_____

_____

_____

_____

_____

_____

_____

_____

_____

_____

_____

_____

_____

_____

_____

_____

Remember when we . . . ?

_____

_____

_____

_____

_____

_____

_____

_____

_____

_____

_____

_____

_____

_____

_____

_____

_____

There was that time we . . .

A great memory!

_____

_____

_____

_____

_____

_____

_____

_____

_____

_____

_____

_____

_____

_____

_____

_____

_____

_____

_____

Remember when we . . . ?

_____

_____

_____

_____

_____

_____

_____

_____

_____

_____

_____

_____

_____

_____

_____

_____

_____

_____

There was that time we . . .

_____

_____

_____

_____

_____

_____

_____

_____

_____

_____

_____

_____

_____

_____

_____

_____

_____

A great memory!

Remember when we . . . ?

_____

_____

_____

_____

_____

_____

_____

_____

_____

_____

_____

_____

_____

_____

_____

_____

There was that time we . . .

_____

_____

_____

_____

_____

_____

_____

_____

_____

_____

_____

_____

_____

_____

_____

_____

A Letter to My Cat

_____

_____

_____

_____

_____

_____

_____

_____

_____

_____

_____

_____

_____

_____

_____

_____

_____

Notes & Fluff

GOOD KITTY

PURR